I0605743

Early
NATURAL DISASTERS
Encyclopedias

WILDFIRES

by Samantha S. Bell

Early Encyclopedias

An Imprint of Abdo Reference
abdobooks.com

abdobooks.com

Published by Abdo Reference, a division of ABDO, PO Box 398166, Minneapolis, Minnesota 55439.
Copyright © 2025 by Abdo Consulting Group, Inc. International copyrights reserved in all countries. No part of this book may be reproduced in any form without written permission from the publisher. Early Encyclopedias™ is a trademark and logo of Abdo Reference.

Printed in China.
102024
012025

Editor: Marie Pearson
Series Designers: Candice Keimig, Joshua Olson
Production Designer: Ryan Gale

Library of Congress Control Number: 2024938386

Publisher's Cataloging-in-Publication Data

Names: Bell, Samantha S., author.
Title: Wildfires / by Samantha S. Bell
Description: Minneapolis, Minnesota: Abdo Reference, 2025 | Series: Early natural disasters encyclopedias | Includes online resources and index.
Identifiers: ISBN 9781098296070 (lib. bdg.) | ISBN 9798384917076 (eBook)
Subjects: LCSH: Wildfires--Juvenile literature. | Natural disasters--Juvenile literature. | Weather--Juvenile literature. | Environmental science--Juvenile literature. | Earth science--Juvenile literature. | Encyclopedias and dictionaries--Juvenile literature.
Classification: DDC 363.34--dc23

CONTENTS

Wildfires can kill even large trees.

Out of Control

A wildfire is a fire that is out of control. It burns wild vegetation. Wildfires can happen anywhere in the world.

Types of Wildfires

There are three types of wildfires. They are ground, surface, and crown fires. Ground fires burn in the soil. The soil has a lot of plant matter, including roots. The fire burns the plant matter. Ground fires can smolder for a long time. They may grow into a surface or crown fire.

Ground fires do not have visible flames.

Surface Fires

Surface fires burn on the ground. They may also burn just above the ground. These fires burn fallen leaves and dry grass.

Crown Fires

Crown fires burn in the canopy. A tree's branches and leaves are its crown. A canopy is the crowns of many trees together. Crown fires burn dead trees and shrubs that stand above grasses.

Dry grasses can catch on fire easily.

Wildfire Types

There are three basic levels of wildfires.

Sometimes there is no wind to make a crown fire spread. These fires are passive. They burn one tree or small groups of trees. Other times, it is windy. Wind makes crown fires active. Fire spreads from one tree to the next through the canopy.

The Fire Triangle

Wildfires need three things to start burning. These are heat, fuel, and oxygen. These three things are called the fire triangle. Heat can come from something natural, such as lightning. It can start with a person lighting a match. Fuel is anything that burns when oxygen is present. Fuel includes wood, leaves, and grass.

Lava can be up to 2,200 degrees Fahrenheit (1,200°C).

Starting a Fire

Fuel comes in contact with intense heat. The heat causes the fuel to react with oxygen in the air. This creates fire. Some wildfires start by natural causes. These include lightning strikes and volcanic eruptions.

Getting Air

Air is about 21 percent oxygen. Most fires need at least 16 percent oxygen to burn.

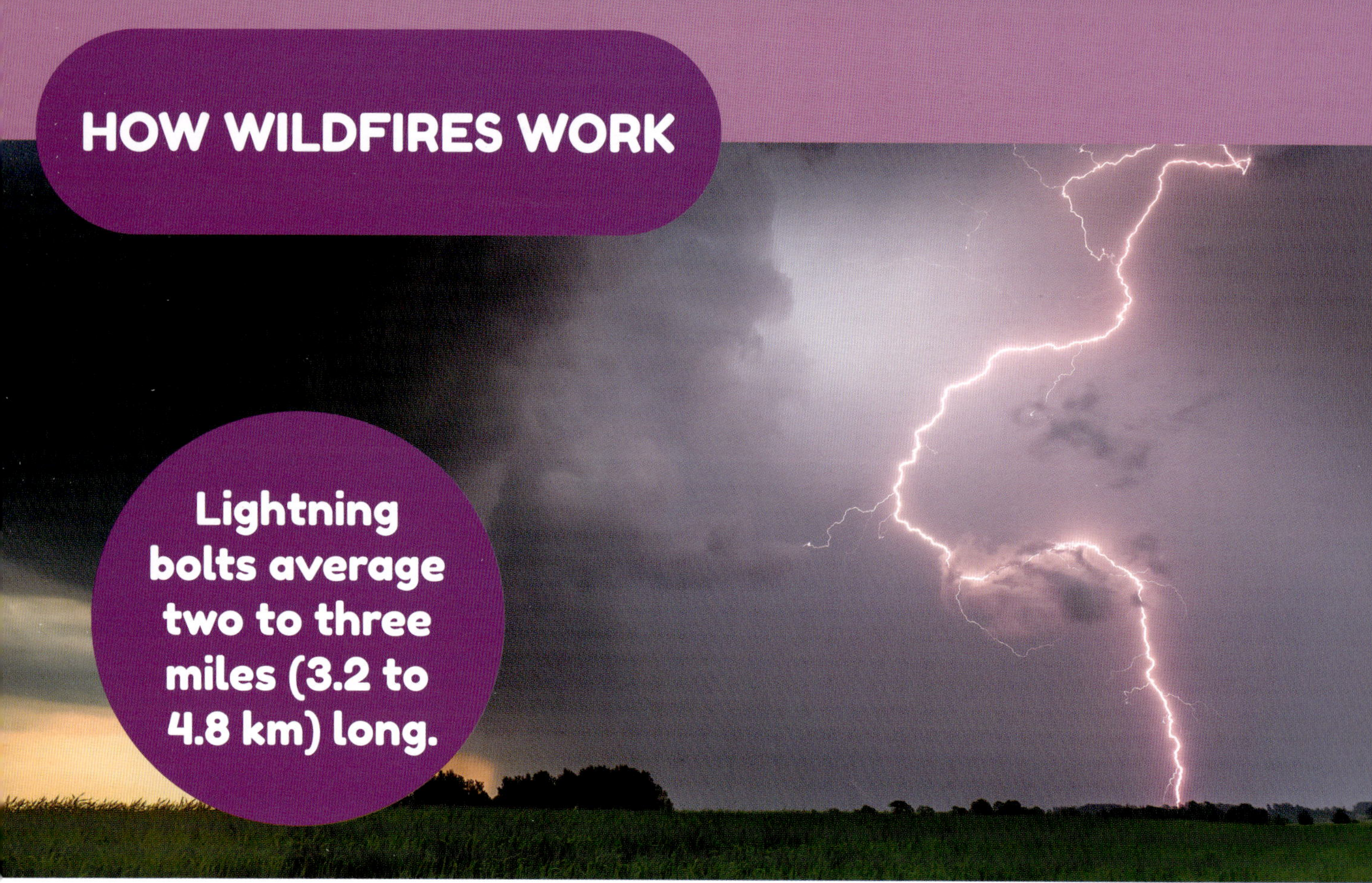

Lightning bolts average two to three miles (3.2 to 4.8 km) long.

Lightning Strikes

Lighting strikes are the most common natural cause of wildfires. Lightning can hit plants. It may hit power cables. This can create sparks that start a fire.

Coal-Seam Fires

There are seams, or layers, of coal in Earth's crust. Sometimes the coal catches on fire. Coal-seam fires can spread to roots in the ground. They start wildfires. Wildfires can also start coal-seam fires.

Spontaneous Combustion

Sometimes fires start on their own. This is called spontaneous combustion. Over time, dead plant matter decays. It can produce heat that builds up. Then a fire may start.

Smoky Mountain in Utah has had an active coal-seam fire for hundreds if not thousands of years.

Fire Seasons

Natural fires happen mainly during certain times of the year. These are called fire seasons. During a fire season, the weather is hot. There is not much moisture in the air. Fuel on the ground dries out. Wind causes fires to spread.

Oklahoma's wildfire season is from November to March.

In 2019, a wildfire burned near homes in Corona, California.

Human Activity

People cause most wildfires. These wildfires can start at any time. They often start when conditions are hot and dry. This causes them to spread quickly. Many start near places where people work and live. These fires can be deadly.

People should keep sparks away from dry plants.

Carelessness

Human carelessness is the main cause of wildfires. People throw lit cigarettes on the ground. They play with fireworks or matches. Sometimes they do not extinguish these items completely.

Dangerous Behavior

People or their activities cause about 85 percent of US wildfires. People cause about 97 percent of the wildfires that threaten homes.

Campfires

Campers often build campfires. Sometimes people leave a fire alone as they do something else. Or they may not put out a fire properly. A fire may look as if it is burned out. But one ember can blow away and start a new fire.

Pouring water on a campfire helps to fully put it out.

Creating Sparks

Certain equipment can create sparks. Chains used to secure items on trailers may drag on the road. Lawn mower blades may hit a rock. These actions can cause sparks that start wildfires.

Lawn mower blades are usually made of steel, which can spark.

Firefighters try to find the place a fire started. This helps them tell if it was arson.

Intentional Burning

People often burn dead leaves or branches in their yards. The fire starts out small. But wind can make it grow into a wildfire. Some people set fire to property such as a building illegally. This is called arson. Arson can also cause wildfires.

Against the Law

People who start wildfires can face severe consequences. They may go to jail. They may have to pay for the damage.

Between 2001 and 2020, the United States had an average of 68,707 wildfires per year.

How a Fire Grows

Some wildfires burn out quickly. Others burn thousands of acres of land. The strength and movement of the fire depends on three factors. These are weather, fuel, and topography. They are known as the fire behavior triangle.

Weather

Certain weather conditions cause a fire to grow. High temperatures and little rain dry out fuel sources. This can cause them to ignite and burn faster. Winds can cause the fire to spread.

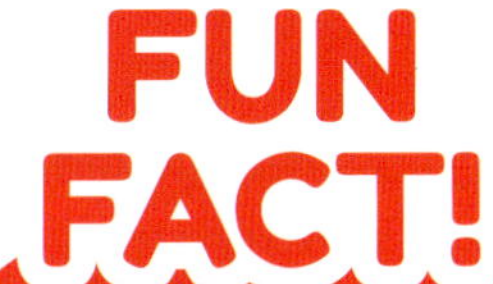

Wildfires usually spread fastest in the afternoon. That is when the air is hottest.

Droughts, which are times of little rain, can dry out plants. Dead, dry plants burn easily.

Strong Wind

Strong winds bring more oxygen to the fire. The oxygen continues to react with the heat. This causes the fire to move at a faster rate. Winds can bend the flames of the fire closer to the unburned fuels. The flames make the fuel lying ahead hotter. This fuel catches on fire more easily.

Wind blew fires through Los Padres National Forest in California in 2021.

Embers are tiny pieces of wood or other burning material.

Blowing Embers

Winds cause embers to blow ahead of the main fire. These reach new fuel sources. They make the fire spread.

Grass burns more quickly than shrubs.

Fuel and Fire Growth

Some types of fuel burn very fast. These include dry grasses, dead leaves, and pine needles. Brush and small trees also burn quickly. These easily burned fuels can spread fire to heavier fuels.

Heavy Fuels

Heavy fuels include stumps, large logs, and heavy branches. These burn more slowly. Fires that involve these fuels are harder to put out. Fire crews might have to break them apart. They must reduce the heat inside.

Fire can travel up the inside of a tree's trunk in addition to spreading from leaves and branches.

Topography and Fire Growth

Topography refers to the land's surface. There are three features of topography. These are slope, aspect, and terrain. Each influences how wildfires spread.

Hills and other features can cause wildfires to move faster in one direction than another.

Slope

The slope of the land is its steepness. It has the greatest effect on wildfires. Fires usually move faster uphill. The flames are close to fresh fuel. The heat dries out the fuel, which then ignites quickly. Also, wind currents normally go uphill. They push the heat from the flames into more fuel.

Sunlight makes water evaporate. So sunny areas are drier than shady areas.

Aspect

Aspect refers to the direction the land faces. Slopes that face the equator receive more direct heat from the sun. These slopes will usually have higher temperatures. They have lower humidity. They also have drier soil and vegetation.

Terrain

Terrain refers to features on the land. These include hills, mountains, lakes, and rivers. They shape the direction of the wind. The wind affects the direction the fire spreads. Bodies of water can provide a gap in fuel sources. This can limit a fire's spread.

FUN FACT!

Wildfires spread at an average of 14 miles per hour (23 kmh).

Fires usually don't burn across bodies of water, but they can if the water is polluted.

Hard to Predict

It is difficult to predict wildfires. This is because people start most wildfires. There is no way to predict what people will do.

Artificial intelligence can spot smoke on cameras. This helps officials respond.

Some fire analysts work for the PG&E Hazard Awareness & Warning Center in San Ramon, California.

Fire Analysts

Once a fire has started, fire analysts work to limit its spread. Some focus on current conditions. They try to predict what a fire might do in the next few days. Others focus on the next few weeks. They want to have a plan no matter what the fire does.

Drought influences how quickly the fuel in an area burns.

Types of Fuel

Analysts consider the types of fuel in an area. Fuel is grouped based on qualities such as size and shape. Analysts think about how much fuel there is. They consider how the fuel is arranged. This helps them predict how fast the fire will burn and how it might move. It tells them how difficult a fire may be to extinguish.

Grass

The first type of fuel is grass. It burns the fastest. The fire spreads quickly. But grass also burns out quickly.

Grass dries out faster than larger plants during a drought, making it more prone to wildfires.

Shrubs

Shrubs include bushes and low-growing trees. The spread of the fire depends on the type of shrub. Some shrubs burn quickly. Others burn more slowly. Slow-burning shrubs may slow the spread of a fire.

Shrubs are plants that are less than ten feet (3 m) tall and have more than one stem.

Dead, dry leaves catch on fire more quickly than branches. The leaves may cause branches to burn that would not have if the branches had been bare.

Faster Flames

The speed at which shrubs burn can depend on the time of year. Trees above the shrubs lose their leaves in the fall. The leaves may collect on the shrubs. This can make the shrubs catch on fire more easily.

Grass-Shrub Fuel

Grass-shrub fuel is a mix of grass and shrubs. Fires with this type of fuel spread quickly with wind but not as fast as with grass only.

Pine needles burn hotter than leaves because the needles are more densely packed on the ground.

Timber Litter

Dead leaves, needles, and twigs on the ground also fuel wildfires. This type of fuel is timber litter. Fires move more slowly through timber litter than grass. They also burn longer.

Ground to the Treetops

Areas may have a large amount of timber litter. This buildup can cause individual trees to catch on fire. Sometimes shrubs act like a ladder. The fire climbs up the shrubs. Then it moves into the crown of a large tree.

Crown fires may burn only a cluster of trees.

Slash-Blowdown

Wind, fire, or snow can break parts of trees. This creates logs, broken branches, and stumps. This type of fuel is called slash-blowdown.

Dead stumps and logs dry out over time.

In some areas, beetles kill large numbers of trees, making them dry and prone to burning.

Burning Slowly

It takes a while for slash-blowdown to catch on fire. The fire spreads slowly. But it burns this fuel for a long time. The fire can be very difficult to put out.

Slash-blowdown fuel also comes from human activities such as road construction and logging.

Fire can jump easily from tree to tree when they're close together.

Horizontal Spacing

Analysts study fuel spacing. Horizontal spacing is how closely the fuel is packed along the ground. Sometimes there is little space between pieces of fuel. Wildfires there can easily spread and grow out of control.

Spread Out

Sometimes the fuel is more spread out. There may be rocks, a stream, or bare ground between fuel sources. These gaps can slow the spread of wildfires. The fires are easier to manage and put out.

Roads can provide spacing between fuel.

Vertical Spacing

Fuels are also spaced vertically. This refers to how they are spaced going up and down. Sometimes fuels are closely spaced. For example, long grass or a shrub may be close to a tree branch. Fire on the grass or shrub can reach the branch. The fire spreads upward. Fuels farther up become heated before they ignite. This makes the fire move even faster.

Fire can work its way from grass to shrubs to trees.

Wind helps fire grow in intensity.

Wind

Analysts also consider the weather. One important factor is wind. Wind is hard to predict. It can change with the shape of the land.

Wind pushes fires in the direction it is blowing.

Wind Patterns

Wind moves quickly up a slope. Wind that goes through a canyon usually moves fast too. It is often turbulent.

Wind and the Environment

Wind also changes with the environment. It slows down if it goes through forests. Wind coming from a body of water usually speeds up. The temperature of the land and water affect the wind too.

The summer temperature of large bodies of water is often cooler than the land temperature, causing wind to form.

Moisture keeps plants healthy and less likely to burn.

Moisture in the Air

Humidity refers to the amount of moisture in the air. High humidity means there is a lot of moisture in the air. Wildfires burn more slowly. Low humidity means there is little moisture. This lets fires burn much faster.

Moisture in the Soil

Moisture is also found in the ground. Sometimes the soil is drier than usual. The area might be experiencing a drought. A drought is when an area is drier than usual for a period of time. The dry, hot weather increases the risk of wildfires.

Plants growing in drier soil than usual have less moisture. They are more likely to burn.

NASA satellites often detect remote wildfires before any other method. They also collect data.

Mathematical Models

Analysts use mathematical models to predict wildfires. A mathematical model is a set of equations. Data is entered into the model. This includes the type of fuel and the amount of moisture. It includes wind speed. The slope and aspect of the land are included too.

Model Information

The model predicts how fast the fire will spread. It tells how intensely it will burn. It also tells where the fire will probably go.

Rothermel's Surface Fire Spread Model

Mathematical models were first used for predicting wildfires in the 1940s. In 1972, an engineer named Richard Rothermel created a new model. His equations are still used today.

The data that analysts gather can be placed on a map that indicates wildfire risks.

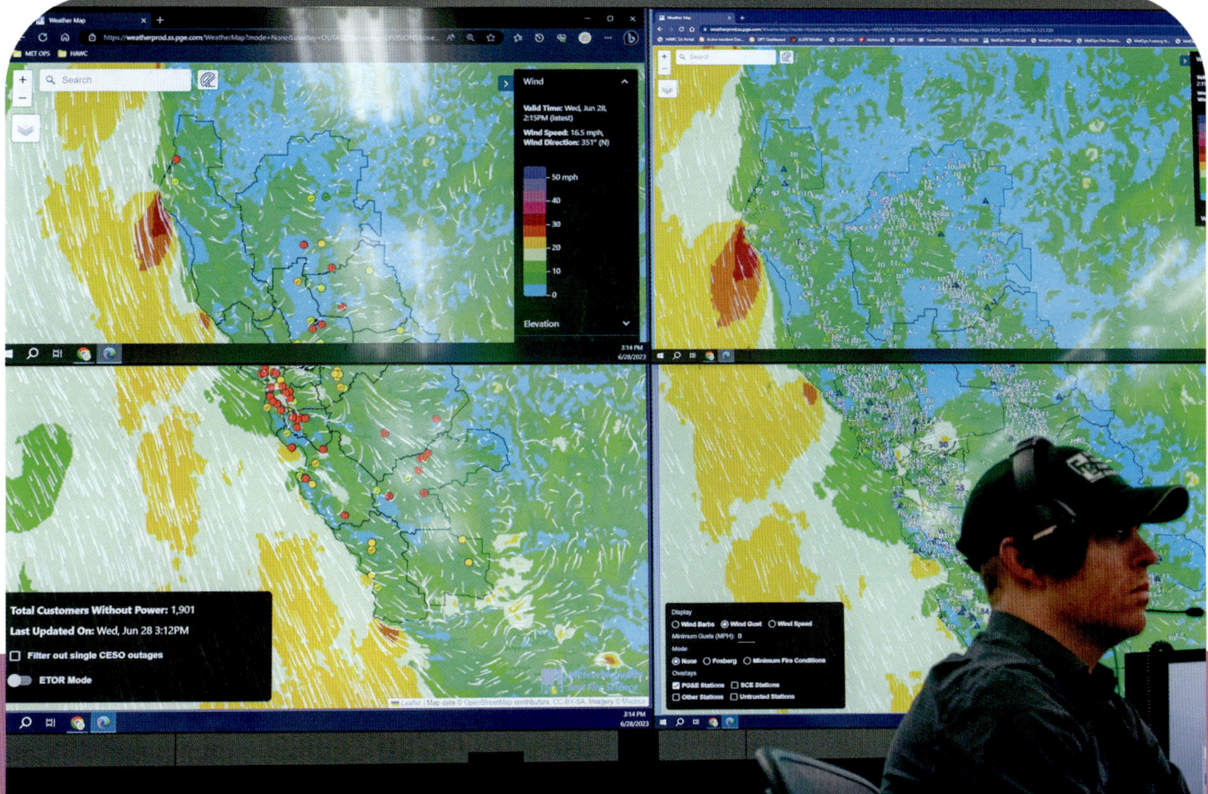

Simulations

A simulation is a model run on computers. It lets analysts see how conditions might affect a fire. It also helps officials decide how to fight a wildfire. For example, sometimes firefighters remove fuel to slow a fire. A simulation can show the best places to do this.

A simulation shows the direction a fire might spread.

Wildfire analysts keep track of a lot of data.

Protecting the Future

Simulations are used for predicting future fires too. Analysts put different forest conditions into a model. The model helps them decide what actions to take to prevent a wildfire.

Natural wildfires in a healthy ecosystem have benefits.

A Natural Occurrence

An ecosystem includes all living things in an area. They interact with each other and their environment. Wildfires are a natural part of many ecosystems.

Keeping Ecosystems Healthy

Wildfires help keep ecosystems healthy. They clear away debris in the forest. Dead or decaying plants build up on the ground. Wildfires make room for new or small plants to grow. They allow sunlight to reach the soil. The sunlight helps the plants grow.

Fertile Soil

Nutrients go back into the soil when plants and animals decay. This happens more quickly if they are burned.

Mugwort grows in an area where the Karuk Tribe held a traditional controlled burn.

Helping Plants

Wildfires are necessary for some plant species to survive. For example, some trees have cones. The cones contain seeds. But the cones are sealed shut with a substance called resin. Wildfires melt the resin. Then the cones release their seeds.

The jack pine is among the trees that have cones sealed with resin.

Birds of prey are among the animals that briefly benefit from wildfires.

Helping Animals

Some animals also depend on fire. They may even go to areas that have just burned. Predators can find prey more easily. There is less shelter for prey.

FUN FACT!

Fires also burn off diseases that harm plants. They kill insects that hurt the trees.

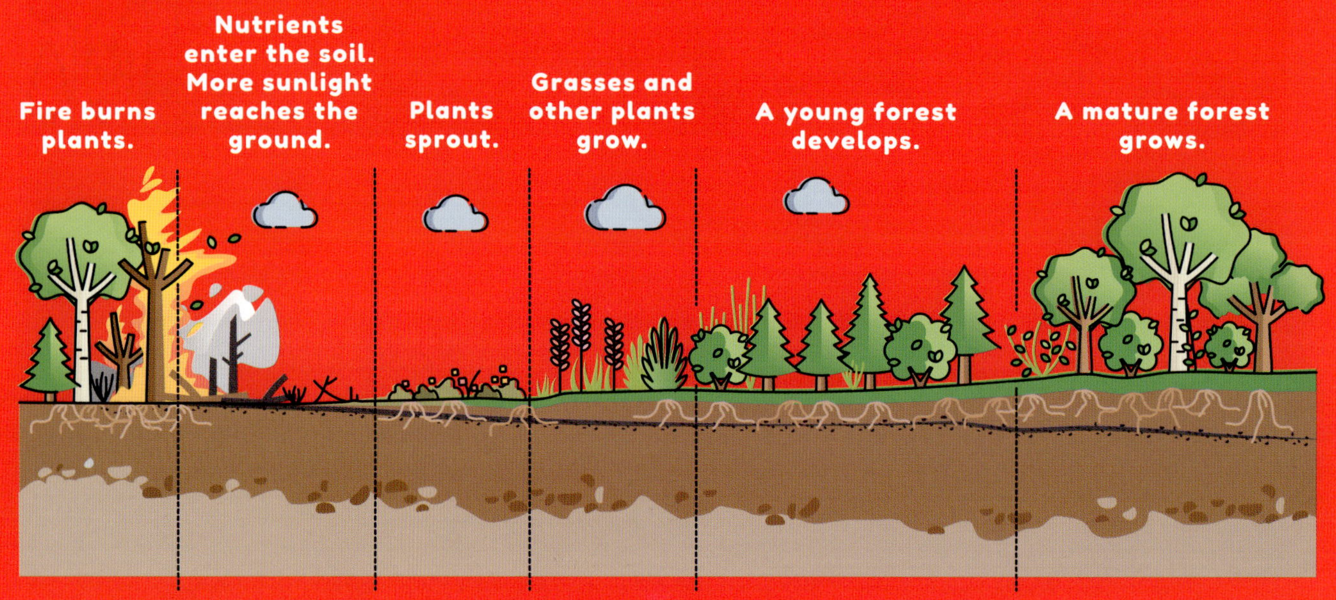

More Food

More light reaches the ground after a fire. The ground is warmer. This is good for lizards. The low plants that grow after a fire are important food sources for some animals. Deer and elk come to graze on the low plants.

Effects on Water

Hot weather heats up rivers and streams. Fish may become stressed or die. But smoke can block sunlight. This helps cool the water.

Invasive Species

Fires can also help remove invasive species. Some invasive species have not adapted to wildfires. Natural species will return. But invasive species may not be able to recover.

Toronto, Canada, is one of several cities that use controlled burns to control invasive species in their parks.

Animals at Risk

Animals can sense danger. Most run away from wildfires. Some stand in streams. Smaller animals hide under rocks. They bury themselves in the dirt.

Forced to Move

Natural wildfires can help wildlife. But intense wildfires can leave animals without homes. Many must search for new habitats. Some animals wander into cities.

A gazelle runs from a wildfire in Turkey in 2023.

Thousands of koalas died in the 2019–2020 Australian fires. Many more needed human care to recover from injuries.

No Escape

Some animals cannot outrun a fire. This includes young, small, or slow-moving animals. These animals may die.

Search and rescue dogs help find people who did not survive wildfires.

Deadly Fires

Wildfires can burn near human communities. Homes can catch on fire. Sometimes people cannot evacuate in time. They are exposed to smoke.

Dangers of Smoke

Wildfire smoke is very harmful to health. Some of the particles are microscopic. People breathe them in. The particles damage the lungs and heart. Wildfire smoke causes more than 300,000 deaths each year.

Wearing masks can help protect the lungs from smoke.

Pets and Livestock

Smoke also affects pets and livestock. The amount of harm depends on an animal's age and health. Animals may cough or pant. Like people, animals can die from breathing in too much smoke.

Plumes of Smoke

Sometimes the smoke from a wildfire forms a tall, thin column. This is called a plume. The plume

Pets may need oxygen if they breathed in too much smoke.

Embers and Smoke

Wind can carry both embers and smoke plumes. The embers can start fires away from the main fire. These are called spot fires. The smoke can travel even farther, causing health issues.

contains tiny particles and gases. These pollute the air. They travel with the wind. They can pollute the air thousands of miles away.

In 2023, a wildfire on the Hawaiian island of Maui burned down entire blocks of buildings.

Loss of Power

Wildfires cause billions of dollars in damages to communities. They burn businesses and homes. They damage power poles. People often lose electricity and cell phone service. This makes evacuations more difficult. It also makes it harder to get help.

Flooding

Plants absorb rainfall. But after a wildfire, there are few plants left. Without them, the soil cannot store the rain. The area floods. Floodwaters damage buildings. Farmers can lose their crops or livestock.

In August 2022, a flash flood swept through an area near Lone Pine, California, that had burned in a wildfire the previous year.

Early Detection

Technology helps detect wildfires quickly. It can find them when they are still small. This helps firefighters stop them from spreading. Technology also helps officials keep track of fires as they burn.

Air quality sensors detect wildfires.

A NASA satellite image shows fires and other hot areas in yellow.

Gathering Information

A satellite is an object in space that circles Earth. Some satellites take photos of wildfires. They gather information. This includes the size, temperature, and location of the fires. All this information helps firefighters know how to respond. Officials can warn people of coming danger.

A thermal image from a drone shows heat from a fire that is otherwise hidden in the trees.

Drones

Drones are aircraft that do not carry people. People control them remotely. Some drones have special cameras that detect heat. They can spot fires.

Internet of Things

The Internet of Things (IoT) refers to devices that share data with each other. They do this through the internet. Sensors on the ground and carried by drone can be part of an IoT system. This system can be spread across a wide area. It creates an early warning system for wildfires in remote areas.

Sometimes military drones are used to help monitor wildfires.

Rating System

The National Fire Danger Rating System (NFDRS) allows US fire managers to estimate the fire danger for an area. This is called the fire danger rating. It is based on weather, topography, fuels, and risks.

Wind is one weather condition considered when fire managers decide on the NFDRS rating.

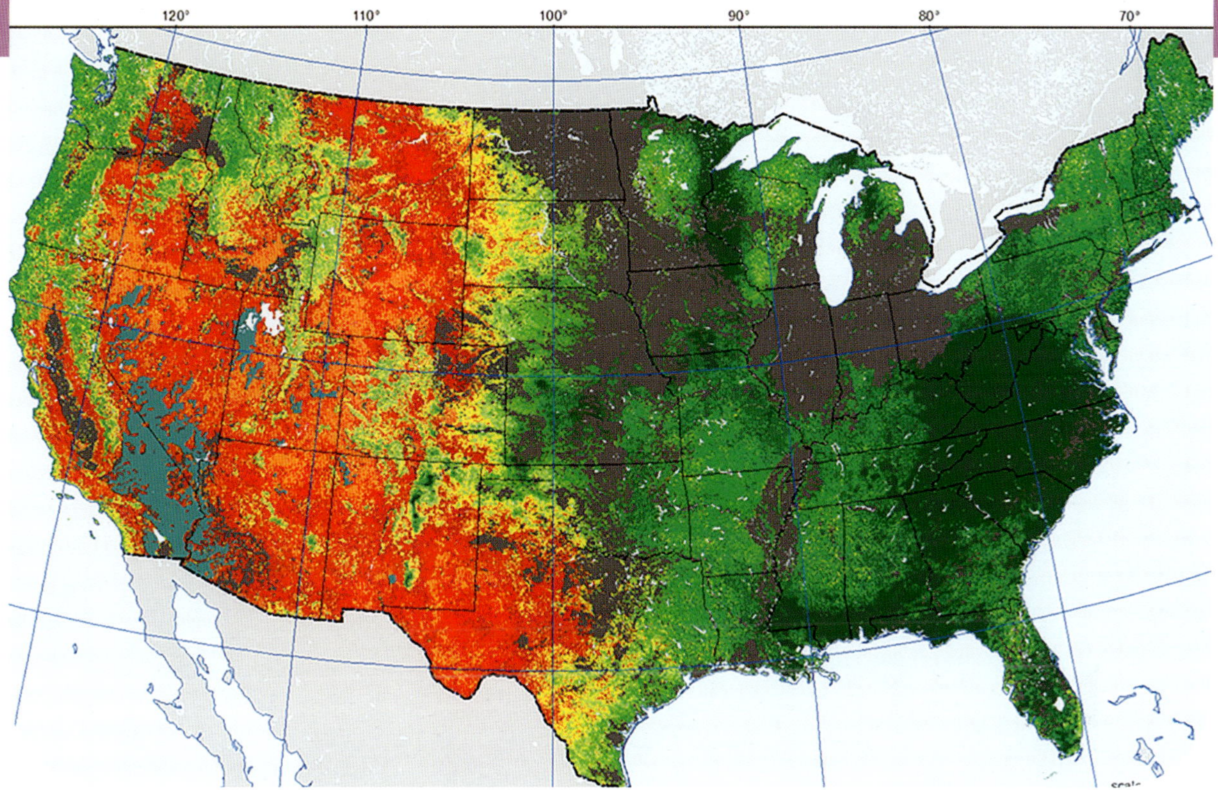

The Wildland Fire Potential Index is another tool that shows the risk of wildfires, with red, orange, and pink being the highest risk of fire.

Fire Danger Ratings

Fire managers determine danger ratings every day during fire season. The ratings describe how fast a fire could spread in a certain area. They help people make decisions about their activities. For example, people may choose not to build a campfire if the danger level is great.

Parks and natural areas may have a sign showing the levels of danger and an arrow pointing to the risk level.

Safer Levels

The Low rating means that fires probably will not occur. If there is a fire, it will be easy to control. The Moderate rating means people can expect wildfires. These fires should be fairly easy to control.

Dangerous Conditions

The High rating means wildfires will probably occur. Very High means fires can start easily. Extreme means any fire that starts could spread quickly and become huge. As these ratings increase, the fires become more difficult to control.

Everyday Actions

When the rating is Extreme, people should not even park on dry grass. A hot car touching the grass can start a fire.

A park may have a fire sign that shows only the day's risk.

Fire Weather Watch

Fire alerts are warnings about possible wildfires. A Fire Weather Watch tells people that coming weather could result in a wildfire. This includes hot, dry weather. It also includes thunderstorms.

Storms can bring rain to put out fires but also lightning to start fires.

Cities put restrictions on certain activities during Red Flag Warnings.

Major Alerts

A Red Flag Warning is more serious. Weather conditions linked to this warning include warm temperatures and very low humidity. They also include strong winds. A Red Flag Warning means a wildfire is likely to occur over the next 24 hours. Everyone should be prepared. The Extreme Fire Behavior alert means that any wildfire that starts will probably burn out of control.

The US Forest Service developed the character Smokey Bear in 1944 to help teach people about wildfires.

Being Prepared for Wildfires

Places where wildfires are likely to happen are called fire-prone areas. People who live in these areas should always be prepared. They should know what the warnings and alerts mean.

Ready to Evacuate

People also need an evacuation plan. They should know where to go. They should take copies of important documents. They should take water and food for several days. They may also need items such as a flashlight and first aid supplies.

People can pack evacuation kits, which include everything they will need while they are away.

Embers and Houses

Homes can catch on fire from flying embers. The embers land on homes. The homes start to burn.

The Danger of Embers

Embers can travel for several miles. Even homes that are far away from the wildfire are at risk. People can do things to protect their homes from burning. This is called home hardening.

Wind can carry embers toward homes.

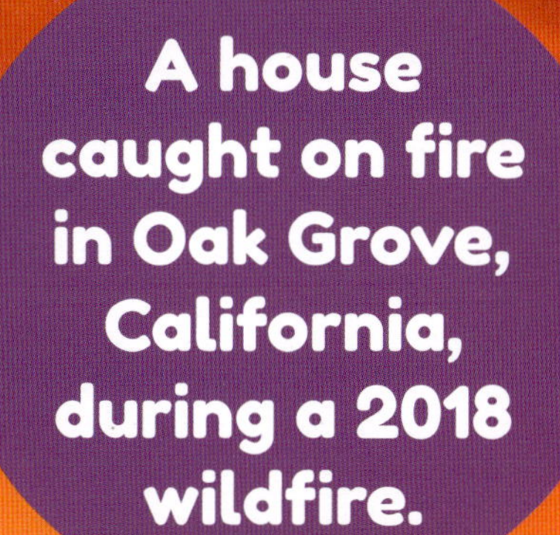

A house caught on fire in Oak Grove, California, during a 2018 wildfire.

Police may go door to door to let people know to evacuate if there is time. People should leave right away to prevent traffic jams.

Creating a Safer Space

Sometimes people cannot evacuate. The roads may be cut off. Or the fire may be moving too quickly. Home hardening can make their homes a bit safer.

Hardening a Home

People should start protecting the outside of the home first. This includes the roof, windows, and siding. It includes the chimney and vents. If embers or flames get inside, the whole house is in danger.

Small buildings such as cabins can be wrapped in aluminum covers to help protect them from wildfires.

Roofs

Some roofs are made of wood or shingles. These are flammable. Roofs in fire-prone areas should be made of fire-resistant materials. These include metal, clay, and tile. People should also keep their roofs clean. Debris such as dry leaves and moss easily catches on fire.

People without fire-resistant roofs may run sprinklers to keep their roofs wet.

Openings

Vents and other openings to the outside should be covered. Otherwise, embers may get inside the home. At least one room should be completely closed off from the air outside. This will help keep smoke out.

Tempered glass is much stronger than other types of glass. If it does break, it is less likely to hurt people.

Windows

Windows can crack from the heat of a fire. They should have two panes. One of them should be made with tempered glass. This glass is treated to resist heat better. Metal screens on the inside help protect homes. If the windows break, embers cannot enter.

Walls and Siding

Wooden walls and siding are more likely to catch on fire. People can replace them with other materials. These include brick and stone. Cement and metal are also safer options than wood.

Preparing the Outside

People can prepare the area around a home to be more fire-resistant. For example, they should clear away fallen leaves. The space within 30 feet (9.1 m) of a home should be cleared.

Clearing the Way

The cleared space will help keep the fire away. It can help slow the spread of a wildfire. This space can also provide firefighters with a safe area in which to work.

Helping the Helpers

People should make sure their house numbers are easy to see from the street. That way, firefighters can quickly find people who call for help.

Clearing the Yard

California requires homes in wilderness areas to follow certain rules.

Zone 0

Five feet (1.5 m): Anything that could catch on fire, such as wooden decks or pine needles, must be removed.

Zone 1

Thirty feet (9.1 m): Firewood and dead plants must be removed.

Zone 2

One hundred feet (30.5 m): Shrubs and trees must have space between them. Grass must be kept no more than four inches (10 cm) tall.

Firefighters use shovels and other tools to make firebreaks.

Keeping Communities Safe

Dealing with wildfires is a difficult job. Firefighters first try to contain a fire. They try to surround it by making firebreaks. A firebreak is an area where there is no fuel. The fire cannot grow.

Making Firebreaks

To make firebreaks, firefighters use hand tools or heavy machinery. They scrape away any vegetation. They may dig a trench. Firefighters may even set a controlled fire to use up the fuel.

Propane torches are commonly used to set controlled fires.

FUN FACT!

Some extreme fires can jump past firebreaks.

Containing Fires

Sometimes a firebreak surrounds a fire. This is called being 100 percent contained. The fire should not spread past the firebreak. But it can continue to burn inside the area.

Firebreaks need to be at least ten feet (3 m) wide.

The average airplane can carry enough fire retardant to fill about five hot tubs.

Slowing Down the Flames

Firefighters also try to remove heat from the fire. They drop water or fire retardant from an airplane or helicopter. These drops cool the fire. They slow it down.

Fire Retardant

Retardant is usually colored red or orange. That way, firefighters can see it easily. They can use it to help create a firebreak.

Drones can carry cameras and other sensors to collect information.

Drones

Using aircraft to fight fires can be dangerous. Pilots may have trouble seeing through the smoke. Drones are safer. They cannot carry a lot of retardant. But they can collect information about the fire. Then firefighters get this information quickly.

Robots

Sometimes firefighters use robots. Some robots drag hoses or spray water. They can find people trapped in burning homes. Firefighters control the robots from a safe distance.

Robots used to fight fires may have tracks instead of wheels. This helps them travel over rough ground.

Returning Home

People should not return home until officials say it is safe. Even then, there may still be dangers to watch out for. These include hot ash and embers. The ground may have pockets of heat. These can burn people. They could also start another fire.

Buildings and streets may be covered in fire retardant when people return home.

Wildfires can destroy almost everything a family owns.

Cleaning Up

Once home, people often have a lot to clean up. Wildfires leave behind a lot of ash. People should wear clothing that protects their skin from the ash. This includes long pants, long-sleeved shirts, and gloves.

Connecting with Loved Ones

Phone systems are often busy after a fire. If there is internet, people can instead use social media to reach out to family and friends.

The gases that make up Earth's atmosphere appear as a blue haze from space.

A Natural Process

Carbon dioxide is a gas. It can be found in Earth's atmosphere. Sunlight warms Earth's surface. Carbon dioxide traps some of the heat, keeping it from escaping to space. In this way, the gas helps keep Earth warm enough for living things.

Changing the Weather

Climate change is a shift in the average weather patterns over time. Too much carbon dioxide leads to higher temperatures. It can also cause longer droughts.

Long droughts can dry up rivers.

Carbon in the Soil

Trees and other plants take in carbon dioxide from the air. When they die, their roots and leaves break down. The carbon dioxide goes into the soil. It is stored underground. Decaying animals release carbon dioxide too.

Plants take in carbon dioxide in a process called photosynthesis. This process is how they make energy to grow.

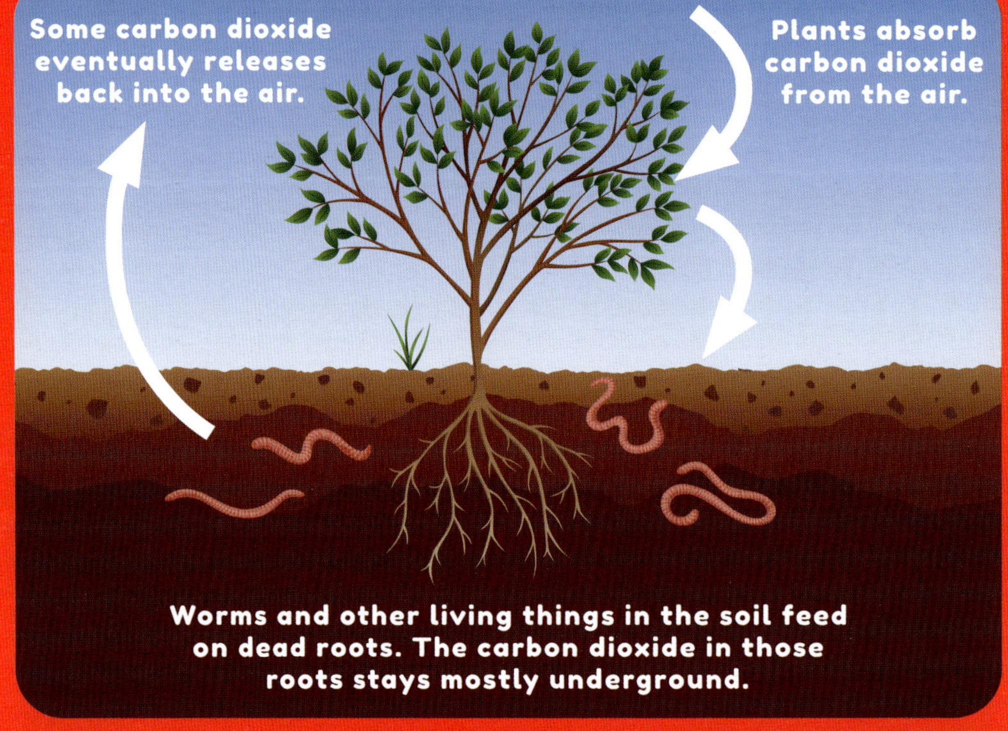

FUN FACT!

There is more carbon in the soil than in the air.

Tree roots extend about two to three times wider than the crown.

Releasing the Carbon

When a wildfire burns, the soil and trees release carbon dioxide. The gas goes into the air. This helps drive climate change.

Growing Fires

The warmer temperatures make fuel drier. This can help fires spread. Warm temperatures make wildfires harder to put out. They can also lead to longer fire seasons.

An Increasing Cycle

Climate change also dries out forests. This causes them to ignite more easily. Larger areas burn. More burning puts more carbon dioxide into the air. This drives more climate change, which dries out the forests more. The problem continues.

A rising number of wildfires contributes to climate change.

Climate Change Fire Cycle

1. Rising temperatures make an area drier.

2. Plants die because of drought. Dry, dead plants catch on fire easily, and the areas that burn are larger.

3. With a wider area burning more frequently, more carbon dioxide is released into the air.

4. More carbon dioxide in the air causes temperatures to rise.

Boreal forests can have many evergreen trees.

Boreal Forests

Today, wildfires happen more often in places where they used to be rare. The boreal regions are in northern areas. They have warm summers and freezing, snowy winters. Climate change is causing these regions to warm up. This makes them more at risk for wildfires.

Rainforests

Rainforests grow in rainy areas. The air has a lot of moisture. Natural wildfires in these places are rare. But people sometimes burn the forests to clear them for other uses. Today, the climate is often hot and dry. The fires people set easily spread.

Rainforests are dense with plants.

Fuel in the Forests

Peshtigo is a town in Wisconsin. In 1871, about 2,000 people lived there. Peshtigo was a logging town surrounded by dense forests. But the loggers left large piles of debris.

Fuel in Town

Mills and factories in the town also produced a lot of sawdust. People stuffed the sawdust under wooden sidewalks. They put it into the foundations of all-wood houses. They layered it in the streets. They left the rest of it in huge piles.

Sawdust is the very small pieces left over from cutting wood.

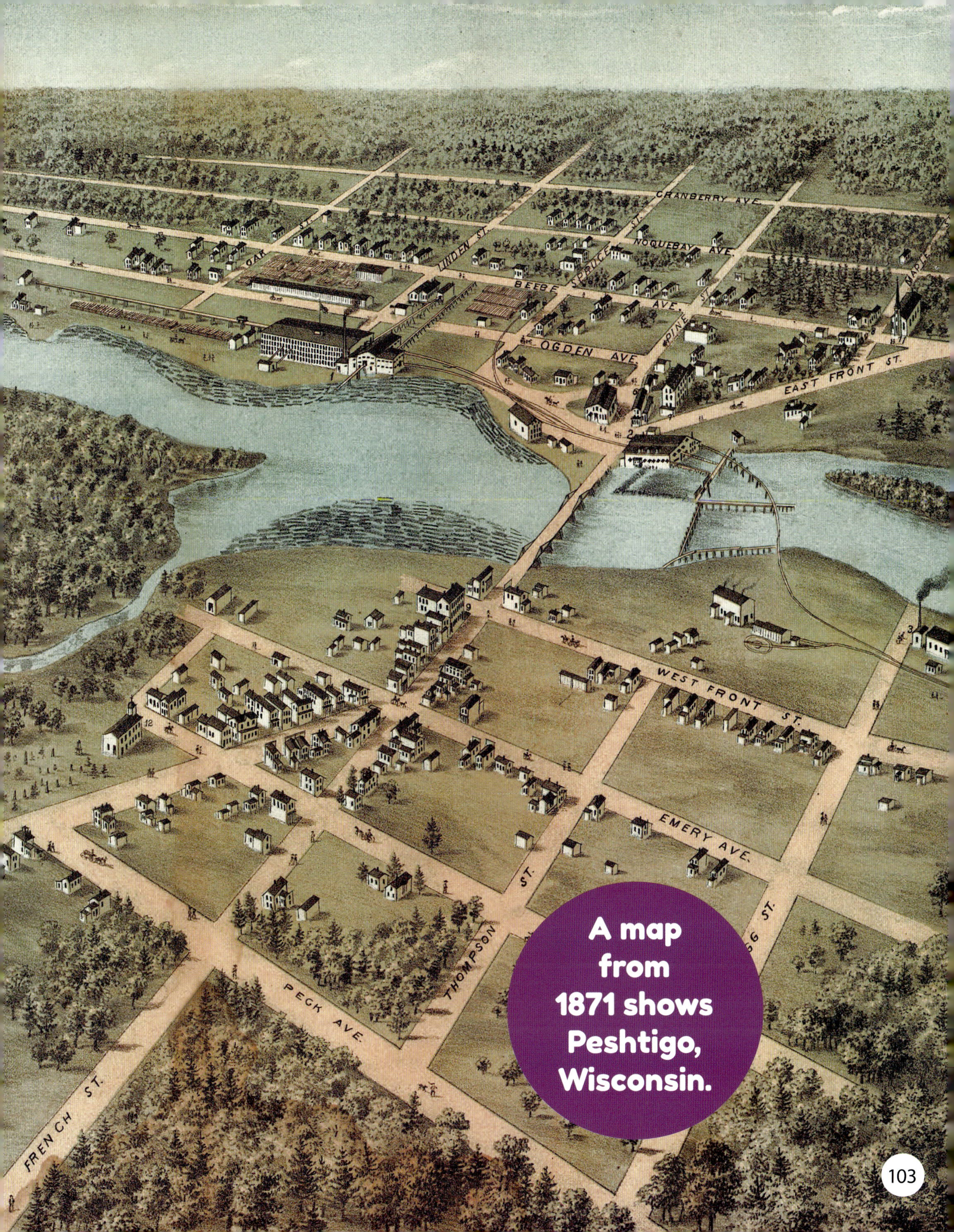

A map from 1871 shows Peshtigo, Wisconsin.

The city of Peshtigo lies on the Peshtigo River. People used this river to move logs.

Setting Fires

Farmers in Peshtigo cleared the surrounding land with slash-and-burn methods. They set small fires to clear the ground. So did the railroad companies. A drought that summer had made everything very dry. Trains threw sparks that often ignited grass fires. Fires were constantly burning.

The Weather

At the same time, there was a long period when temperatures were higher than usual. When cooler temperatures came, they produced winds. The winds whipped the small fires into a massive one.

FUN FACT!

Peshtigo is called the City Rebuilt from Ashes.

With so much wood at the sawmills, there was plenty of fuel for the fire.

A Tornado of Fire

On the night of October 8, 1871, winds whipped up to 100 miles per hour (160 kmh). They stirred up the fire even more. Cool air caused a huge column of hot air to rise. This produced more wind. It became a whirlwind of fire.

When wind whips fire into a tornado, it is called a fire whirl.

The Peshtigo Fire Museum includes a Bible and china dishes that were damaged in the fire.

No Time to Escape

The wind threw fencing, railroad cars, and even whole buildings into the air. The fire moved fast. Building after building caught on fire. Many of them burned before people could get out. Peshtigo was completely destroyed.

Fast Destruction

The fire continued to burn until it reached the waters of Green Bay. Then the storm winds died down. Rain came and put out the fire. In two hours, the fire burned more than 438 square miles (1,130 sq km) in eight counties.

A wood engraving made in 1872 shows people attempting to flee the fire.

A Great Loss of Life

Some people survived by going into the Peshtigo River. Others went down into wells. But 800 people in the town died. About 700 people from surrounding towns also died in the wildfire. It remained the deadliest wildfire in US history more than 150 years later.

Queensland firefighters worked to put out bushfires in 2019.

Bushfire Season

Wildfires are common in Australia. They are called bushfires. Queensland is a state in the north of Australia. It had severe bushfires starting in 2019.

Ready for Fire

Fires in Queensland usually begin in August. But in 2019, the first major bushfires started in June. There had been several years of drought. Fuels were dry. Temperatures were also higher than average.

Orchard farmers in Queensland lost trees to the drought in 2019.

New South Wales

Two states in southern Australia also had severe bushfires. One of these was New South Wales. On October 26, a lightning strike started a huge fire. Over the next few months, many more bushfires started.

A satellite captured images of smoke from 2019 bushfires in New South Wales.

November fires in Victoria burned large areas of land and destroyed homes.

Victoria

The other southern state was Victoria. On November 21, conditions were ideal for wildfires. The government of Victoria imposed a total fire ban. No one could start a fire out in the open. But that same day, three lightning strikes started bushfires. By the end of the day, 150 fires were burning in the state.

The Fires Continue

By December, which is summer in Australia, nearly 100 fires were burning across New South Wales. That same month, almost 200 new fires broke out in Victoria. The fires continued to grow and spread. They destroyed homes and killed livestock. Other states also fought bushfires. These included the Australian Capital Territory, Western Australia, and South Australia.

Relief

Rains in January 2020 brought some relief. But hotter temperatures and high winds caused the fires to spread again. Finally, a very heavy

Megafires

Many fires in New South Wales and Victoria burned fast and were very intense. They became known as megafires.

rainstorm helped firefighters contain all the fires in New South Wales by mid-February. The last of the fires in the country were finally put out or contained in Victoria by March 4.

Australia Map

Australia has six states and two major mainland territories in addition to smaller territories and those located farther away.

Many people in Australia lost property and loved ones.

Dangerous and Deadly

The most intense bushfires produced huge plumes of smoke and ash. The plumes rose up to 19 miles (31 km) high. Thirty-three people died from the fires. The smoke caused hundreds more deaths.

Vast Destruction

In all, about 65,600 square miles (169,900 sq km) of land burned. Approximately three billion animals were killed or forced to move to new locations. More than 3,000 homes were destroyed.

The ash from the bushfires drifted to New Zealand and turned its glaciers brown.

Wildlife rescuers saved animals such as kangaroos during the wildfires.

Dry Thunderstorms

California is the most fire-prone US state. On August 16 and 17, 2020, intense thunderstorms rolled in. More than 15,000 lightning strikes started fire after fire. Warm winds followed the storms. They blew the fires in all directions. Within three days, there were more than 350 fires.

Lightning struck near San Francisco on August 16, starting fires.

Soldiers from Wisconsin were among the people who arrived to help with the wildfires.

The August Complex

The fires merged. When this happens, the fire is called a complex. The California fire became known as the August Complex. It was so large that state officials had to call for help from other states.

Firefighters battled a fire in Jamul, California, in September 2020.

Burning for Months

In early September, there was a record-breaking heat wave. Winds stirred up more fires. The August Complex fire continued to burn until November 12, 2020. Firefighters were still working to contain other fires in December.

Thousands of Fires

By the end of the year, nearly 10,000 fires had burned in California. More than 6,600 square miles (17,100 sq km) burned. This included groves of giant sequoias and ancient redwoods. It was the largest wildfire season recorded in California's modern history.

The fires blackened the trunks of towering sequoias.

Fighting Fire from the Air

California has the most firefighting aircraft in the world. The state used 132 aircraft when the fires were at their worst. The planes brought 11 million gallons (41.6 million L) of retardant. The helicopters dropped more than 18 million gallons (68.1 million L) of water.

California used 44 airplanes and 88 helicopters during the 2020 wildfire season.

San Francisco's sky was orange on September 9 because of the smoke.

A Sky Full of Smoke

For weeks, plumes of smoke went into the atmosphere. The smoke was so thick in some places that it blocked out the sun. It made the sky appear dark orange. It could even be seen from space.

The American Red Cross set up shelters for people who lost their homes.

Dangerous Particles

Tiny particles traveled through the air. They were very dangerous to breathe in. The particles affected people who lived hundreds of miles away.

Far-Reaching Effects

The fire crossed seven counties. More than thirty people lost their lives. This included three firefighters. Officials believe that thousands more died from breathing in the smoke.

People posted signs thanking firefighters for their bravery and sacrifices.

GLOSSARY

controlled fire
A fire that is planned and managed.

decay
To break down into smaller parts.

ember
A small piece of material that is burning.

extinguish
To stop something from burning.

fire-resistant
Describing something that does not catch on fire easily.

fire retardant
A material that can slow or stop the spread of fire.

flammable
Something that catches on fire easily.

ignite
To cause to start on fire.

invasive species
Plants or animals that do not originally belong to a certain environment.

microscopic
Something that is too small to see without special tools.

smolder
To burn slowly without flames.

turbulent
Very rough.

vegetation
The plants growing in an area.

TO LEARN MORE

More Books to Read

Griffey, Harriet. *Earthquakes and Other Natural Disasters*. DK, 2023.

London, Martha. *Wildfires*. Abdo, 2020.

Murray, Julie. *Smokejumpers*. Abdo, 2021.

Online Resources

To learn more about wildfires, please visit **abdobooklinks.com** or scan this QR code. These links are routinely monitored and updated to provide the most current information available.

INDEX

PHOTO CREDITS

Cover Photos: Shutterstock Images, front (firefighter, wildfire), back; Morakot Kawinchan/Shutterstock Images, front (helicopter)

Interior Photos: Shutterstock Images, 1, 3, 4, 7 (nature), 7 (fire), 8, 9 (bottom), 11, 14 (top), 14 (bottom), 17 (bottom), 18, 19, 21, 23, 25, 26, 33 (top), 33 (bottom), 34, 35, 36, 38, 47 (top), 50, 51 (top), 53, 54, 55 (top), 61 (background and trees), 61 (fire), 61 (grass), 61 (smoke), 61 (city), 71 (top), 71 (bottom), 74, 75, 76, 81, 82, 83 (house), 83 (vent), 84, 85, 89 (bottom), 93 (bottom), 96 (plant, soil, sky), 97, 99 (trees), 99 (fire), 100, 114; InciWeb, 5; Lutsenko Larissa/Shutterstock Images, 6; Ammit Jack/Shutterstock Images, 9 (top); Kaspars Daleckis/Shutterstock Images, 10; Eugene R. Thieszen/Shutterstock Images, 12; Tim Gray/Shutterstock Images, 13; Trusova Evgeniya/Shutterstock Images, 15; Gino Santa Maria/Shutterstock Images, 16; Mel Melcon/Los Angeles Times/Getty Images, 17 (top); Al Seib/Los Angeles Times/Getty Images, 20, 86, 121; A. Lesik/Shutterstock Images, 22; Josh Edelson/AFP/Getty Images, 24, 93 (top); Anton Starikov/Shutterstock Images, 27; Patrick T. Fallon/AFP/Getty Images, 28, 48; Justin Sullivan/Getty Images News/Getty Images, 29; Jeffrey B. Banke/Shutterstock Images, 30; George Trumpeter/Shutterstock Images, 31; Andrew Orlemann/ Shutterstock Images, 32; Bishal Napit/iStockphoto, 37; Bai Xuefei/Xinhua News Agency/Getty Images, 39; Fabrizio Maffei/Shutterstock Images, 40; Brenton Geach/Gallo Images/Getty Images, 41; Erin Donalson/ Shutterstock Images, 42; Serghei Starus/Shutterstock Images, 43; Nik Merkulov/Shutterstock Images, 44; Jason Salmon/Shutterstock Images, 45; NASA, 46, 65, 94; Jason Henry/Bloomberg/Getty Images, 47 (bottom); David Paul Morris/Bloomberg/Getty Images, 49; Carlos Avila Gonzalez/San Francisco Chronicle/ Hearst Newspapers/Getty Images, 51 (bottom), 68, 118; Lukas Gojda/Shutterstock Images, 52; Mert Alper Dervis/Anadolu/Getty Images, 55 (bottom); Sergen Sezgin/Anadolu Agency/Getty Images, 56; Lisa Maree Williams/Getty Images News/Getty Images, 57; Ricky Carioti/The Washington Post/Getty Images, 58; Lev Radin/Shutterstock Images, 59; Mustafa Ciftci/Anadolu Agency/Getty Images, 60; Mario Tama/Getty Images News/Getty Images, 62; David McNew/Getty Images News/Getty Images, 63, 79, 80, 92, 106, 122; Matthias Bein/dpa/picture alliance/Getty Images, 64; Oak Ridge National Laboratory/US Department of Energy, 66; Cpl. Emmanuel Necoechea/US Marine Corps/DVIDS, 67; US Geological Survey, 69; Norm Lane/Shutterstock Images, 70; David McNew/AFP/Getty Images, 72; Paul Chinn/San Francisco Chronicle/Hearst Newspapers/ Getty Images, 73; Wally Skalij/Los Angeles Times/Getty Images, 77; Trevor Bexon/Shutterstock Images, 78, 125; Sgt. 1st Class Steven Eaton/US Army/DVIDS, 87; Cpl. Brandon Martinez/US Marine Corps/DVIDS, 88; J. M. Eddins Jr./US Air Force/DVIDS, 89 (top); Peter Thomson/La Crosse Tribune/AP Images, 90; Shen Diancheng/China News Service/Getty Images, 91; Mike Dotta/Shutterstock Images, 95; Marina Akinina/ Shutterstock Images, 96 (worms); Vladimir Ya/Shutterstock Images, 98; R. P. Baiao/Shutterstock Images, 101; Germanova Antonina/Shutterstock Images, 102; Library of Congress, 103; The Print Collector/Hulton Archive/Getty Images, 104; PL Photography Limited/SuperStock, 105; Stacey Wescott/Chicago Tribune/TNS/ Sipa USA/Alamy Live News/Alamy, 107; Red Line Editorial, 108, 115; iStockphoto, 109; Daniel Taylor Producer/ Shutterstock Images, 110; William West/AFP/Getty Images, 111; Orbital Horizon/Copernicus Sentinel Data/ Gallo Images/Getty Images, 112; Brook Mitchell/Getty Images News/Getty Images, 113; Saeed Khan/AFP/ Getty Images, 116; John Moore/Getty Images News/Getty Images, 117; Spc. Michael Ybarra/US Army/DVIDS, 119; Sandy Huffaker/AFP/Getty Images, 120; Jessica Christian/San Francisco Chronicle/Hearst Newspapers/ Getty Images, 123; Gabrielle Lurie/San Francisco Chronicle/Hearst Newspapers/Getty Images, 124